An essay on credit and the Bankrupt Act. With some reflections on the Escape-Act.

An essay on credit and the Bankrupt Act. With some reflections on the Escape-Act.
Multiple Contributors, See Notes
ESTCID: T089549
Reproduction from British Library
Text is continuous despite break in pagination.
London : printed, sold by A. Baldwin, 1707.
[2],vi,61,[2],62-78p. ; 8°

Gale ECCO Print Editions

Relive history with *Eighteenth Century Collections Online*, now available in print for the independent historian and collector. This series includes the most significant English-language and foreign-language works printed in Great Britain during the eighteenth century, and is organized in seven different subject areas including literature and language; medicine, science, and technology; and religion and philosophy. The collection also includes thousands of important works from the Americas.

The eighteenth century has been called "The Age of Enlightenment." It was a period of rapid advance in print culture and publishing, in world exploration, and in the rapid growth of science and technology – all of which had a profound impact on the political and cultural landscape. At the end of the century the American Revolution, French Revolution and Industrial Revolution, perhaps three of the most significant events in modern history, set in motion developments that eventually dominated world political, economic, and social life.

In a groundbreaking effort, Gale initiated a revolution of its own: digitization of epic proportions to preserve these invaluable works in the largest online archive of its kind. Contributions from major world libraries constitute over 175,000 original printed works. Scanned images of the actual pages, rather than transcriptions, recreate the works *as they first appeared.*

Now for the first time, these high-quality digital scans of original works are available via print-on-demand, making them readily accessible to libraries, students, independent scholars, and readers of all ages.

For our initial release we have created seven robust collections to form one the world's most comprehensive catalogs of 18th century works.

Initial Gale ECCO Print Editions collections include:

History and Geography
Rich in titles on English life and social history, this collection spans the world as it was known to eighteenth-century historians and explorers. Titles include a wealth of travel accounts and diaries, histories of nations from throughout the world, and maps and charts of a world that was still being discovered. Students of the War of American Independence will find fascinating accounts from the British side of conflict.

Social Science
Delve into what it was like to live during the eighteenth century by reading the first-hand accounts of everyday people, including city dwellers and farmers, businessmen and bankers, artisans and merchants, artists and their patrons, politicians and their constituents. Original texts make the American, French, and Industrial revolutions vividly contemporary.

Medicine, Science and Technology
Medical theory and practice of the 1700s developed rapidly, as is evidenced by the extensive collection, which includes descriptions of diseases, their conditions, and treatments. Books on science and technology, agriculture, military technology, natural philosophy, even cookbooks, are all contained here.

Literature and Language
Western literary study flows out of eighteenth-century works by Alexander Pope, Daniel Defoe, Henry Fielding, Frances Burney, Denis Diderot, Johann Gottfried Herder, Johann Wolfgang von Goethe, and others. Experience the birth of the modern novel, or compare the development of language using dictionaries and grammar discourses.

Religion and Philosophy
The Age of Enlightenment profoundly enriched religious and philosophical understanding and continues to influence present-day thinking. Works collected here include masterpieces by David Hume, Immanuel Kant, and Jean-Jacques Rousseau, as well as religious sermons and moral debates on the issues of the day, such as the slave trade. The Age of Reason saw conflict between Protestantism and Catholicism transformed into one between faith and logic -- a debate that continues in the twenty-first century.

Law and Reference
This collection reveals the history of English common law and Empire law in a vastly changing world of British expansion. Dominating the legal field is the *Commentaries of the Law of England* by Sir William Blackstone, which first appeared in 1765. Reference works such as almanacs and catalogues continue to educate us by revealing the day-to-day workings of society.

Fine Arts
The eighteenth-century fascination with Greek and Roman antiquity followed the systematic excavation of the ruins at Pompeii and Herculaneum in southern Italy; and after 1750 a neoclassical style dominated all artistic fields. The titles here trace developments in mostly English-language works on painting, sculpture, architecture, music, theater, and other disciplines. Instructional works on musical instruments, catalogs of art objects, comic operas, and more are also included.

The BiblioLife Network

This project was made possible in part by the BiblioLife Network (BLN), a project aimed at addressing some of the huge challenges facing book preservationists around the world. The BLN includes libraries, library networks, archives, subject matter experts, online communities and library service providers. We believe every book ever published should be available as a high-quality print reproduction; printed on-demand anywhere in the world. This insures the ongoing accessibility of the content and helps generate sustainable revenue for the libraries and organizations that work to preserve these important materials.

The following book is in the "public domain" and represents an authentic reproduction of the text as printed by the original publisher. While we have attempted to accurately maintain the integrity of the original work, there are sometimes problems with the original work or the micro-film from which the books were digitized. This can result in minor errors in reproduction. Possible imperfections include missing and blurred pages, poor pictures, markings and other reproduction issues beyond our control. Because this work is culturally important, we have made it available as part of our commitment to protecting, preserving, and promoting the world's literature.

GUIDE TO FOLD-OUTS MAPS and OVERSIZED IMAGES

The book you are reading was digitized from microfilm captured over the past thirty to forty years. Years after the creation of the original microfilm, the book was converted to digital files and made available in an online database.

In an online database, page images do not need to conform to the size restrictions found in a printed book. When converting these images back into a printed bound book, the page sizes are standardized in ways that maintain the detail of the original. For large images, such as fold-out maps, the original page image is split into two or more pages

Guidelines used to determine how to split the page image follows:

- Some images are split vertically; large images require vertical and horizontal splits.
- For horizontal splits, the content is split left to right.
- For vertical splits, the content is split from top to bottom.
- For both vertical and horizontal splits, the image is processed from top left to bottom right.

AN ESSAY ON CREDIT

AND THE Bankrupt Act.

WITH SOME REFLECTIONS on the Escape-Act.

---

*How can a gen'rous Freeborn Mind
Assist a Tyrant, that Mankind
Of Native Right deprives?
But in Mankind's Defence to waste his Blood,
To Perish nobly for the Publick Good,
Sure such a Death is worth a Thousand Lives!*
                    [Thanksgiving ODE.

LONDON,
Printed, Sold by A. Baldwin in Warwick-Lane, 1707.
Price One Shilling.

AN ESSAY ON CREDIT AND THE Bankrupt Act.

WITH SOME REFLECTIONS on the Escape-Act.

*How can a gen'rous Freeborn Mind
Assist a Tyrant, that Mankind
Of Native Right deprives?
But in Mankind's Defence to waste his Blood,
To Perish nobly for the Publick Good,
Sure such a Death is worth a Thousand Lives!*
　　　　　　　　　[Thanksgiving Ode.

LONDON,
Printed, Sold by A. Baldwin in Warwick-Lane, 1707.
Price One Shilling.

TO

Samuel Shepard, Esq;

Member of Parliament for the CITY of *London*.

SIR,

YOU have the Honour to Represent in Parliament the greatest City in the Christian World, and it's an Honour to them to have such a Representative.

So great a Body, Composed of such mighty Different Members, will always be doing Mischief to its self, by hurting each other,

TO

Samuel Shepard, Esq;

Member of Parliament for the CITY of *London*.

SIR,

YOU have the Honour to Represent in Parliament the greatest City in the Christian World, and it's an Honour to them to have such a Representative.

So great a Body, Composed of such mighty Different Members, will always be doing Mischief to its self, by hurting each other,

other, if the Head Calms not their Debates, Reconciles their Opinions, or Over-rules them to their own Interest.

To you therefore do I present the following Sheets, to state the Debate fairer before you than it has yet probably been; that you may Convince your Fellow-Citizens how much more it's their Interest to Cure, than to Cut off a Diseased Member from their Body.

Thus, Sir, as you have managed with unequal Applause, the Affairs of the greatest Society in our Isle, and penetrated so far into its Interest, that every one was better pleas'd you should manage it than themselves, I hope they'll pay that Deference to your Judgment, as to lay aside their Prejudice

Dedicatory.

judice against the Reasons which are offered to them, if they are approved by you.

Then shall *London* shine with a double Lustre, for She seems only to encrease in Wealth, when She decreases in People: And tho' She could reckon up many *Claytons*, *Duncombs*, *Jefferies*, and *Scawens*, She will insensibly decay if She Glories only in Her Mighty Citizens, and neglects Her Poor Ones.

Her Sisters in *Holland* herein Exceed Her, who grow Greater whilst She's at best but at a Stand; and it seems Reserved for you to Teach Her Her True Interest.

So shall you out-shine the *Greshams* or *Suttons* She boasts of, and I shall be very Happy in having any hand in Exciting one so able

able as you to do such Services to my Country.

Sir, The Parliament's being already on this Subject, I shall keep you no longer from it, but submit intirely to your Examination, whether the Abuses complain'd of against this Act be Real or Imaginary? or whether either sort may not be Remedied in whole or in part? or whether making the Bill Consistent with its self, by which I mean so certain, that all that run away shall be Hang'd if they are Caught, and all that Surrender Clear'd, if nothing is made out against the Truth of their Discovery, be not infinitely preferable to all the Old Laws against Bankrupts?

For those, Sir, who have already surrender'd, as they are Objects of Mercy, the Parliament

Dedicatory.

ment only can Relieve them; and I must particularly Recommend them to you to plead their Cause, it's the Cause of the Poor and Needy: By such Actions, Sir, the Antients form'd their Glory, and by such, Sir, you'll leave a Name Equal to theirs, if you Exert your self, and shew that Vigour and Resolution that has so Eminently appear'd in you on many Occasions. And every one will follow such a Pattern, or at least cease to be Ill when you are so exaltedly good.

I, Sir, shall not go without my Share of Glory, by singling out so able a Patriot, who, as soon as any thing Great or Charitable is Recommended to him, undertakes it with a Joy equal to those that want it, without any private Interest or Friendship; for the

World may see by this Epistle you have not seen it, nor know the Author for any other than one of them that has a high Opinion of you, and who is

Sir,

Your Most Humble and

Most Obedient Servant.

AN ESSAY ON *Credit* and *Bankrupts*.

THERE is so much more difficulty in defending than accusing the Unfortunate, th t I am satisfyed who ever will please to be so Ill-humoured, as to find fault with me for this Essay, will find it very easy.

There are so many Rogueries daily committed by Men of all Degrees and Employments; and a *P-tk-n* and his Accomplices, are Villains so much more pernicious than the Man on the Black Mare, that were it ever allowable to Condemn the Innocent with the Guilty, or were it possible one Man would venture to Trade were all Bankrupts to be hang'd, I believe many would desire all should.

And

An ESSAY on

And among them, some that may be ~~so themselves, as there were~~ that opposed the last Bankrupts Act, who have already wanted the Benefit of it; for such a Spirit of Cruelty reigns here in *England* among the Men of Trade, that is not to be met with in any other Society of Men, nor in any other Kingdom of the World.

A Bankrupt, is a Trader, made unfortunate by some Loss or Disappointment, which he often can neither help nor foresee, and which cannot be his Fault, he having neither the Command of Winds or Convoys, nor the certain Knowledge of the Circumstances of those he Trusts.

But being a Bankrupt, a Cry arises against him, Commissioners, Messengers, and other Limbs of the Law, bring mighty Statutes to prove their Right (like the Lyon) to the biggest share of him, and if he prove but a little Morsel, to all. For when the Goods are sold, at 3 or 400 *per Cent* Loss, and the Sittings, Assignments, &c. are pay'd, very little comes to the the Creditors, who being thereby more incensed, worry their Brother Trader

Trader, till they Nail him in a Jail, make him Transport himself, or see him in a Grave, and never think he was one of them, and that they may feel the Chains they make him wear.

Thus their Misfortunes name them Bankrupts, than which nothing can be more Ignominious. How different are Soldiers that Chance to be Unfortunate? if they are killed in Fight they die in the Bed of Honour; if they lose a Leg or an Arm, their boldly venturing in their Calling, makes their being Cripples very far from a Disgrace; or if their Regiments are broke, they Command every ones Wishes till they are provided for again.

When neither Storms, nor Shipwracks, Fire nor Water, nor Mischief in all the various Shapes War shews it in, can beget Pity to the Wretch that feels them all.

But here I must do that Justice to all other Nations, that I know none of them guilty of this Crime.

France with its despotick Power, is kinder to its People in this particular than we are; and when their Traders are unfortunate, their Effects are divided

vided among their Creditors; out of which he has a share, to take Care of his Family.

Holland believes that every Trader is a part of the Commonwealth, whatsoever be their Circumstances; and like a Mother extends her Care to all her Children, and lets none be made useless. She knows, she cannot make Men pay when they han't it, and gives them time; and that her Rasp-houses; are made for Criminals, not Debtors none of whom are ever Confined, but at the Creditors Charge, nor then, if it appear they are unable to pay. And

Scotland, like Her, allows time to them that want it; and if the Creditors by any means fasten on their Debtors they must maintain them, in proportion to their Rank; which if they do not weekly, the Prisoner is *ipso facto* Discharg'd.

In Denmark, Sweden, and the Wise State of Venice, their Grandees Protect their Insolvents; and all the World finds the Advantage of mildly treating them, few ever being found, who were not really so, who would Sacrifice their

their Credit and hopes of future gain, for a Protection: Which when Men really want, its evidently better, both for the State and their Creditors, to let them have, then to drive them away: by which the first lose so many People, and the last their Debts.

Which Protection the Unfortunate here in *England* found from her Peers, all the time of their Power; but as that declin'd, and wore away by degrees, they gathered themselves into Places which they call'd Priviledg'd: But which soon grew very odious and scandalous; for how could they be otherwise, when fill'd by People, hated by God and Man; miserable distressed Creatures, reduc'd to Starving or Villany; for Necessity makes as many Rogues, at least, as Nature, who rather than Starve, will do any thing to prevent it; and are less to be blamed, than the many *Spadilio*'s we Daily see, whom the ingenious Doctor *Garth*, mentions in his incomparable Poem.

Spadilio, *that at Table serv'd so late, Drinks rich Tockay himself and Eats in*
(*Plate*;
Has

Has Levees, Villas, Mistresses in Store,
And owns the Racers, which he rubb'd be-
(*fore.*

Who continue when so raised, without the excuse of Necessity, to draw in our Young Nobility and Gentry into their Nets by the vilest ways, who set them, share them, and rob them, first of their Estates, and then of their Principles, by perswading them to join with them to recover their Losses, till the Estates of the one, and the Rank of the others, makes the vice so Epidemical, that it is too big for the Legislature to hope to Reform. The modish Pick-pockets grow so exalted, they Rival the Dukes they Converse with, and these Mushrooms believe themselves their Equals; for they having suffer'd them to Play with them, in good Manners bear with them in every thing, tho' they are perfectly acquainted what every one loses by it but themselves; and which can never be remedy'd, till a Genius big with the good of *England,* glorious for being so like my Lord *Sommers* in Counsel, or the Duke of *Marlborough* in the Field, shall rouse the Spirits of our Nobility with their Ancestors, or their own Glory,
and

and fire them with Indignation against these Locusts, which prey upon them, and who ought to be Branded to all Posterity.

But to return from this Digression to the Houses of the Unfortunate, I can think it no Wonder, when a thousand Tricks were found to be daily Committed there, that appear'd naked, ungilded, and wicked, that an Act of Parliament was obtained to suppress the Places.

But had the Miserable any Advocates, or the Unfortunate Friends, to have stated their Case before Condemnation, some saving Clause might have been found, to distinguish the Innocent from the Guilty, which might have remov'd the Cause of what was so complain'd of.

By forcing them to Pay who had any thing to do it with, and by discharging them that did so; and by Relieving them who had nothing at all; but the Prosecution ended not here, but after several Attempts, which from Year to Year were made vain by Parliamentary Mercy, they obtain'd, by their

their perpetual Clamours against the Insolence of their Debtors, an Act to punish Escapes.

And tho' I will freely own it very provoking for a Man to see a Debtor, who he had made a Prisoner in the Fleet or Queen's-Bench, come out of the Rules of the Prison, and perhaps Buy and Sell, without paying his Debts; and answer when ask'd for it, 'The Law had taken its Course, and 'that he will not be teiz'd; or that he 'can pay but so much in the Pound, 'which he will not part with, till 'every one agree to it: It's no wonder if such Answer, indifferently worded, in return to Reproaches heavily enough laid on them, inflam'd their Creditors so to Revenge, that the Punishment was only regarded, and the Remedy again overlook'd that should cure the Cause.

For neither was the Evil so great as it seem'd, either that Prisoners should go out of the Rules to Buy or Sell, or give their Creditors such Answers.

The Reason the Queen's-Bench and Fleet have several Streets allow'd them, for

for their Prisoners to live in, call'd by that name, is, because since it's become the Custom to put Debtors in the Prisons of Criminals, the Houses are uncapable to hold the twentieth Part of them, and the County Allowances and collected Charity will not keep their Tenths with the Bread and Water of Affliction, so that they must have larger Places to hold them, and liberty to get Bread for themselves, for which however their Goalers will be Paid.

Neither can it be expected they should pay any Part of their Debts, till they can be discharg'd from the whole; for if an Insolvent cannot perswade his Creditors to accept of a Composition, when he offers them his All, they who refuse that, to be sure, will never discharge him when he has nothing left to pay them.

Yet this colour'd over, begot the Escape Act, which was oftner refus'd than any Act that perhaps ever pass'd, and is certainly the severest that ever was Enacted, at least that hath been so long unrepeal'd.

B   The

The Reasons gave for it I have shown, the Pretences for it were those Reasons dress'd in all the Forms Losers could put them in against Men they lost by, many of whose Characters deserv'd a Punishment, which fell as well on others that did not.

A Punishment quite different from all others in the World.

It does Good to no Man.

It prevents not the Evil for which it's Inflicted, which is the design of all Penal Laws.

It punishes pure Misfortune severer than the highest Crimes committed by Man against one another, or against the Government, nay even against God.

It's no advantage to him that Inflicts it, the nailing a Debtor to the Prison Walls till he dies, pays him not a Farthing of the Debt, and is so far from doing him any good, that it makes his other Religion of no u'e, while he is so far out of Charity with his Brother.

And

And I am perswaded if such a Man had liv'd when Christianity was in its Glory, and its Discipline rever'd, the Holy Communion would have been refus'd to Men so Inexorable, who Sacrifice harmless Infants to their violent Resentments; and it's as certain as our Holy Religion is true, that their's can profit them nothing, in which Charity has no Part.

But the Severity of perpetual Imprisonment in this Case is not *ad Exemplum*, we would not by it restrain Credit, or fright People from trusting their Effects to Seas and Factors.

Our Trade is so much abroad our Glory and our Strength, and we find it so impossible to maintain our selves, preserve our Navigation, and consequently our Liberties without it, that it could not be design'd as a *Memento*, to forewarn Men of running any Hazards, lest that should be their End; for by this Law, no Man that Trades can please himself, that his Honesty will secure him from so dreadful a Fate.

The Captain of any Ship, or a principal Servant, that will betray his Trust, as well as the Seas, the Winds, a Pirate, or Fire at home, may thus reduce the uprightest Man alive, and Immure him, not between two, but a Hundred Thieves, and the difference between them, is only to his disadvantage; for they are not, as he, Excluded from the Mercy of the Throne.

The Queen, like God, who she represents, takes no Pleasure in punishing her Subjects, and often on Representations, that there's hopes the Condemn'd Malefactors are Penitent, and may mend, lets them taste of her Mercy, and after Sentence of Death, forgives them all their Crimes; thus there's no Criminal but may sue for a Pardon from God and his Vicegerent on Earth, save the Insolvents took up by this Act, who are miserable beyond all Example, for they alone cannot be Reliev'd from the Throne.

If it seems strange, that the Legislature has not been Deafned with their Cries, who can hear them through Stone Walls? who can they ask to carry up

their

their Petition? who will deliver it? who will Plead their Cause against their Adversaries? who will Labour for them without hopes of Return? and how can they Answer Accusations they know not, or Reasons they hear not? Or can Justice alone help them against such Odds? had they Pity to joyn with them? Could their Miseries be seen, were they to creep out of their Cages, their Wants like the Darkness of *Egypt* would be felt, and they could not fail of being Reliv'd; for were they allow'd to Plead, they might say with the *Hebrew* Queen on another dreadful Occasion, to the *Persian* Monarch, That if they, their Wives, and Children were only to Perish, or to be Sold for Bond-men and Bond women, or much worse, to be Immur'd for Life, they should not deserve notice, if the Damage was not as considerable to the Nation as the Punishment is severe to them.

There not being a Ship lost, the Consequences of which does not affect abundance of Men; the Owners and Freighters are far from being the only Sufferers; the numerous Trades that fit out a Ship, and every Shopkeeper or Artificer they buy of, must follow their Merchant's Fate, they cannot Pay if they are not Paid; what muſt they then do? Either be ſued till they ſurrender in diſcharge of their Bail, and then live there, till having ſpent all, they are caught abroad ſolliciting an Agreement with their Creditors, who perhaps ſeize them doing ſo, or in providing Bread for their Families, for whom a *Gehenna* on Earth is prepar'd.

They that will not expoſe themſelves to this Riſque, when they find themſelves Inſolvent, run away, and tho' they have enough to pay fifteen Shillings in the Pound, and ruin no Man, knowing it next to impoſſible to get every Creditor to agree, they either go away with it to other Nations, who grow richer by our Labour, by our Manufactures, and by our People; or if they ſtay at home, hide all Day, and do worſe at Night, and leave their Children to the Pariſhes to maintain, till the poor Rate ariſes to be a Tax greater than any laid on for the War.

And a Man no ſooner becomes a Priſoner in diſcharge of his Bail, than he falls to work to make Money of

every

every thing that can be turn'd into it, and then leaves the Kingdom to avoid that Act. Thus as the Loss is very great by the Effects annually carried away, and which never return, the number of People is as considerable a Loss. And if the Judges were order'd to lay before the Parliament an Accompt how many Yearly have turn'd themselves over since the Escape Act, who were never thence discharg'd, so very few of whom in Proportion remain in their Prisons; we should find so many Families lost by it, and such a Stock probably carried away; besides those greater Numbers aforemention'd, who will not stand so long.

If there was no Mercy due to them as they are Miserable, or as our Brethren, the Interest of the Nation would repeal that Act, and I cannot but hope, this Sessions that fatal Bill will have its Period.

And the City of *London* this last Session prepar'd the Bankrupts Bill in hopes it would remove the Cause.

Nothing was so reasonable, as that Fraudulent Bankrupts should be Punish'd, nish'd; and the way to do it, was to Relieve them that were Honest; for it's equally reasonable, that every Bankrupt should deliver to his Creditors what is none of his own, as that he should be Discharg'd that does so: The whole World will adjudge that Man to the Gallows, that uses his Credit with his Neighbour on purpose to get his Goods, and run away with them; and he will equally deserve it, that because a Loss happens to him, runs away with his All, and leaves nothing to his Creditors; but then he must be Discharg'd on his fair Delivery.

And an eminent Member for the City of *London* shew'd so much Religion in his Anger at the Malice of some that were unwilling to discharge the Debt, on the delivery of the Effects. It ought to be remember'd for his Glory, and I hope he'll live to see the good Effects of what he had so considerable a hand in; for I will venture to say, that this Act, when explain'd and amended, or something it will produce, will answer most of the Ends the Nation groans for, relieve the Wretched that call for it on Heaven,

ven, save a multitude of Families, by dividing among them the Bankrupts Estate, before they have spent it in keeping off the Evil Day; for tho' 'tis the Opinion of many, and of several of good Sence, that Creditors are willing to accept of what their Debtors can offer them, the cause of that Opinion is, either that they are themselves willing, or that they think others are so because they ought.

For if they would look for Examples, which is the surest Guide, they'd find, that for one who refuses to pay his Creditors a Composition in his Power, and which all would agree to take, twenty are at least kept in Jayls by some obstinate Creditor, who resolving not to be satisfied with his Share, compleats the Ruin of the Bankrupt, and prevents other Creditors Receiving a Dividend they might have had, which they see afterwards spent; from whence arises that common Speech so well known among Traders, *That the first Offer is always the best*. And I might add as many more are willing to Pay what they can, than do endeavour to Cheat their Creditors by a Reserve: That many more Instances can be given

of

of Bankrupts, who on their Composition offer and undertake to pay more than they are able, in hopes that Providence, or their Diligence, may make it up to them.

By this time it may be objected, if the Bankrupt's Bill is so good, from whence comes the Complaints against it, which every where is met with?

The Answer to which I would give with that Candour, that the Truth may so Evidently appear to all who look for it, as to perswade such Gentlemen, who have neither Friends nor Relations any way concern'd in Affairs of Trade, to afford a little time to Regulate it for the Advantage of the Kingdom in General; in which the greater their Estates are, the greater is their Share.

The first, and great Objection against the Bill, is, that Payments are made in Affidavits; that the Bankrupt has his Debts discharg'd, but the Creditors get nothing.

This being certainly true, it must occasion a world of Complaints: It's so

natural

natural for Mankind to be Angry with them they suffer by, that it would be no less than a Miracle, if on this occasion they lost their Resentments: And if by Computation Four Hundred poor Bankrupts that were thoroughly Reduced, have one with another Twenty Creditors, there are Eight Thousand Complainants; and Creditors of Twenty or Forty Shillings, or such trifling Summs, are often harder to be satisfyed, than Creditors of an Hundred Pound; for they care not whether they lose their Debts or no, they won't abate a Farthing to a Rogue that would cheat them, when a considerable Creditor is willing to take his Share, because he wants it.

And if we imagine these Eight Thousand dispersed, as they are, up and down the Kingdom, telling their Neighbours when they read the Gazettes, that such and such a Rogue, (their Language for Debtors) are come off without paying them a Groat, we may see very plainly this occasions the Complaints.

But when, in the other Scale, I put the Bankrupt's Answer, That Lawyers,

yers, Bailiffs, and Jayl-Keepers, have fleec'd them, that they have been perhaps strugling for Liberty many Years, and have paid to several of their Creditors part of their Debts in hopes of it; and that all that while they and their Families could not be Fed without Victuals, or subsist without Lodging and Cloaths, which being out of Business, must consume the rest.

The Creditors themselves must confess their Poverty; and it's well known many of them have begg'd by Ten or Twenty Shillings, Thirty Pound, the Price of their Redemption.

This being fairly stated, the Gentlemen whose Complaint I Allow'd, and whose Anger I Excus'd, will find themselves in the whole not hurt by this Bill.

Three or Four Hundred are discharg'd by it, and their Creditors got nothing of them, that had nothing to deliver; but the Debt is not made a bad one by it, it was equally so before; for he that has nothing can pay nothing; and Men of Rank, for their own Characters will not pretend it's any Damage

mage to themselves, or the Nation, that they, who have nothing but their Hands or their Trades to provide for themselves and Families should be allow'd to use them.

Hence the general Clamour arose; And the Bankrupts of Twenty Years, finding nothing required by this Act but an honest and fair Delivery, fling in their Mite, which was all they had left, like the Woman in the Gospel, and hop'd their Creditors would by the Divine Example, see they should be satisfied with it: For had there been a Clause in the Act, to have put to Death all those Bankrupts who had nothing left, either to live on, or to deliver; which had been much kinder, than either to have forgot them, or left them out to starve, there would have been many Traders that had not dislik'd this Bill; for the Dividends that have been made of them, whose Misfortunes bear a fresher Date than the Twenty Fourth of *June*, are so much above what was ever known, that as they feel the Good of the Act, they cannot help being pleased with it; for there can be no such Proof of the Goodness of any Law, as that both Parties gain by it.

The

The honest Trader may sleep with Safety, without the Fear of a Prison, which is much more dreadful than of a Storm, when he knows that if the hand of God falls on him, he shall not, which is much worse, fall into the hands of Men, or have occasion to bail Action after Action, to hunt for Sham Pleas, or bring Writs of Errour, and then buy off one to pay another, so to maintain a Running Fight, in hopes it may last till he is sav'd by Death: And Credit will have another Face when it's known that Buyers are not worse than nothing; and if a Misfortune makes them so, the Creditor can but lose his Proportion; which generally will be very small; and good Money will not then be flung after bad, which has so much been a Custom, and so long complain'd of.

But as the proportion of six Months is to Twenty Years, so are the Numbers of them that love the Bill out of Interest, and hate it out of Anger; for the Bill is as yet known but as Experience teaches.

I have, indeed, heard it complain'd that some Bankrupts have made private

Pay-

Payments to their Friends, before the issuing of their Commissions, that destroyed the Design of the Act, which was an equal Dividend.

But as I am not yet come to offer the Remedy on the part of the Creditor, I shall as yet only look on what occasion'd this Corruption, which avoiding for the future, the Evil in a great measure may be prevented.

For the Usage of Bankrupts, who fairly surrender'd, was so Cruel, and their Hardships so unsupportable, that it's rather a Wonder every one did not run into this Fault, than that some few did.

As the Act pass'd the Commons House, he that made a Delivery as directed, had nothing to fear; he knew he was a Felon or Free, that the Account he gave in was at his Peril, and he was to die if it was false; but the Clamour of them that oppress'd the Bill, begat a posthumous Clause, for which there was no Provision in the Act, which else would have been a very good one.

The

The honest Trader may sleep with Safety, without the Fear of a Prison, which is much more dreadful than of a Storm, when he knows that if the hand of God falls on him, he shall not, which is much worse, fall into the hands of Men, or have occasion to bail Action after Action, to hunt for Sham Pleas, or bring Writs of Errour, and then buy off one to pay another, so to maintain a Running Fight, in hopes it may last till he is sav'd by Death: And Credit will have another Face when it's known that Buyers are not worse than nothing; and if a Misfortune makes them so, the Creditor can but lose his Proportion, which generally will be very small; and good Money will not then be flung after bad, which has so much been a Custom, and so long complain'd of.

But as the proportion of six Months is to Twenty Years, so are the Numbers of them that love the Bill out of Interest, and hate it out of Anger; for the Bill is as yet known but as Experience teaches.

I have, indeed, heard it complain'd that some Bankrupts have made private
Pay-

Payments to their Friends, before the issuing of their Commissions, that destroyed the Design of the Act, which was an equal Dividend.

But as I am not yet come to offer the Remedy on the part of the Creditor, I shall as yet only look on what occasion'd this Corruption, which avoiding for the future, the Evil in a great measure may be prevented.

For the Usage of Bankrupts, who fairly surrender'd, was so Cruel, and their Hardships so unsupportable, that it's rather a Wonder every one did not run into this Fault, than that some few did.

As the Act pass'd the Commons House, he that made a Delivery as directed, had nothing to fear; he knew he was a Felon or Free, that the Account he gave in was at his Peril, and he was to die if it was false; but the Clamour of them that oppress'd the Bill, begat a posthumous Clause, for which there was no Provision in the Act, which else would have been a very good one.

The Act directed a Man on the third sitting to deliver his all, and that being his last Act of Conformity, it was reasonable he should.

But had the last Clause been in View, that a Bankrupt after his full and fair delivery of his Effects, must stay three Weeks for my Lord Keeper, to see if any will oppose him, and then perhaps six more for to come to the Judges, and must get Council for hearing after hearing, to the most frivolous Objection, it cannot be supposed they would have stript a Man so Naked, and turn'd him loose to be Worryed by any Creditor, when the Means is in their Hands which should defend him, and when he has nothing left to subsist on.

Thus the Design of the Act is again perverted: For who can fight with Hunger, and what Man is there who had made ever so fair a surrender, who would not after his delivery give fresh Bonds and Judgments to any Creditor, that would oppose him, **when** the Alternative was starving, if **he did** not, unless he had more F iends **than** the Unfortunate could hope for.

For

For as it could not be design'd by them that made the Law, that a Man should first give up all his Effects, and be thus forc'd to renew the Debt, which the delivery was to satisfie; it may easily be supposed, that when this Practice obtain'd the other soon followed.

And that Men before they broke would make some Friend, who in Humanity would be oblig'd to support them, from the Day of their Delivery, till the gaining their Certificate.

Thus every Bankrupt was within the Power of their Creditors, and the very threatning of a Petition to Men they knew had no Money to oppose them, was like clapping a Pistol to the Breast to force them to whatever they pleas'd; and they whose Friends stood by them in the evil Hour, had generally the additional Misfortune to tire them out without Advantage to themselves.

And here I am oblig'd to Name the Judges, for whose Body I have a mighty

mighty Reverence, and that high Regard for some of them, who are adorn'd with all the Vertues we can wish for on the Bench, that no Man can more admire them; yet they shine with a different Light as one Star out Shines another, and the best and greatest of them are but Men liable to Mistakes.

And this being the Foundation of Appeals, I hope none of them will take it more amiss, my differing in some things with some of them, than they do the Gentlemen of the Law, who by Arguments seem to Labour to bring them to their Opinion at the Bar; and often not without Success, which I mention to their Glory, which it's certainly more to be convinced than to be obstinate in the Wrong.

And its very certain, the cry against Bankrupts, and against the late Act, had made a mighty Impression on them.

Every Man that was angry, that his Debtor was like to get off, raved against the Bankrupt and the Act.

The Act they condem'd, the Bankrupt they loaded with all the Names of Infamy

famy and Reproach, which reach'd the Judges, but not their Answers to them, it's no wonder therefore they came too often (I mean some of them) to the Bench of Justice, full of Zeal, to prevent the Roguery of Bankrupts; for they had a Notion that all Bankrupts were Rogues.

Some indeed declar'd, they sat as Judges of Equity, and that if a Bankrupt deliver'd up his all, he could do no more, and his Creditors could have no more, and that the Law design'd such Men a Discharge, and that if the Act was dubiously worded, it was meant and should be so explain'd.

But the Majority was of another Opinion.

The Letter of the Law clear'd those, who after the Twenty Fourth of *June* became Bankrupts, within any of the Statutes against Bankrupts, who should do as the Act directed.

The Act was to prevent Frauds, to force every Debtor to deliver whatever he had to his Creditors, on the

Terms

Terms of Liberty, and Men of no Principle would not accept of Liberty on thoſe Terms.

And the very Man, who was Conſiderable enough to be nam'd by the Committee of the Houſe of Commons, as not to deſerve the Benefit of the Act, would not accept of it; he would neither deliver what he had to his Creditors, nor venture to ſave any thing at the Riſque of Death, and they that honeſtly deliver'd, did compleat their own Ruin.

If a Commiſſion is took out againſt a Bankrupt, after the Twenty Fourth of *June*, and he ſummon'd, or notice given him to ſurrender, as directed by the Act, on the penalty of Death, What muſt he do? Tho' he had committed Acts of Bankrupcy before, he muſt be Conſcious of committing them ſtill, and if it can be prov'd, that after the Twenty Fourth of *June*, a Commiſſion was iſſued againſt him, and that he committed after that Day one Act of Bankrupcy, within any of the Statutes againſt them; ſhould he not ſurrender as by this Law is directed, I believe every one, would have Condemn'd him to the Penalty of it; for my part, had I been on such a Jury, I should have look'd on him as a fraudulent Bankrupt, and such a Pretence but an Evasion.

This I may be sure of, that much more honesty was shewn by them that made a fair discovery, and they deserve Mercy much more than if they had not.

The Judges have indeed at last given it as their Opinion, that once a Bankrupt and always so, and that any Act of Bankrupcy committed before the Twenty Fourth of *June*, excludes the Bankrupt from any Benefit from this Law, though he had since that Day committed new Act of Bankrupt, within several Statutes which he had not before: Thus he that has surrender'd on the Summons of the Law submitted to the Penalty of it, and has a Certificate from the Commissioners delegated by my Lord Keeper, of the Truth of his delivery and his conforming to every part thereof, has no Benefit thereby.

The Judges own'd that such Deliveries deserve a Discharge, and that it's hard the Honest should not have it; but they thought the Act not plain enough to impower them to sign Certificates in these Cases.

And some who have surrender'd to this Act, merited nothing by so doing; and it unfortunely happen'd, that one of the greatest Abuses of it, was attempted on a Person whom the whole World admires, and who none but a Rogue of the first Form durst venture, or could hope to Cheat, which being publick, furnish'd every Body with Complaints.

And the Council against the Bankrupt might well alledge, that from the Bench to the Stall it encourag'd Wickedness: And as such a Story fill'd common Ears with Indignation, it must fix a general ill Opinion of People in the same Circumstances, as if Guilty of the same Crimes.

That Great Man himself well knew it was no more possible the Bankrupt Act, tho' ever so good, could exclude all Knaves the Advantage of it, than

that

that the perfect Knowledge of the Law could be a Security not to be cheated by one who will stick at nothing: For as the Benefit of the Sun and Moon, the Rain and the Dew from Heaven, are equally given and Enjoyed by the Worthy and Unworthy, so *Magna Charta*, and every Law of our Land extends without Exception to all.

Thus the Faults of some few Persons that have sought for Advantage by this Bill, and the Clamours against the Act for them, are of no Weight, tho' Cloath'd in a Pompous Dress, and Adorn'd with all the Flowers of Rhetorick. And even the Bankrupts might very easily Recriminate on that Noble Body which is made up of all our Lawyers, if Crimes committed by any Member of them were a Reflection on all.

And were it not for the Respect due to those Gentlemen of the Long Robe, who in every Age have been Advocates for Liberty, and whose great Learning stem'd the Tide of Tyranny, the happy Effects of which we now enjoy.

And for those numerous worthy Patriots, who in this Age are a Glory to their Profession, and Equal the greatest of their Predecessors, so many of whom precede on the Bench, and so well fill their Places, in either House of Parliament, or at the Bar, I should have but a mean Opinion of the pleading part of a Profession that generally confounds Right and Wrong, and pleads each Cause with the same Warmth and Zeal.

An Exalted Merit may pick and chuse its Causes; and a *Sommers*, a *Cooper*, a *Hales*, and a *Holt* at the Bar might refuse to plead on the unjust side, the World knew their Worth, and they had not the fewer Causes for the many they turn'd off.

And a *Montague*, a *King*, a *Parker*, a *Raymond*, and another *Cooper*, with many others, may do so still.

But what Numbers plead without distinction, who by false Colours pervert Justice, and with their silver Tongues so adorn an ill Cause, that Right is overcome, the Owners dispossess'd of their Estates, and the Children sent a Begging, while others enjoy them,

till

till it's become a Proverb, *The Longest Purse always prevails.*

But is not every thing to be said for ones Client?

No, The speaking for Money can never excuse what ought not to be said without it, and waving the Irreligion and Woes denounced against Lawyers, for such Practices, the Immorality of the Tongue, that perverts Justice, and triumphs over Truth, is as flaming, as if they themselves were principle, nay worse, for the smallness of the Temptation adds to the Sin; and for a hundred Guineas what Wrongs do they not plead for, and often succeed in, which their Client would not have done for a few Thousands?

The taking Fees, in the same Cause, on contrary sides, on different Occasions: The giving Opinions to please the Enquirer, to draw him into a Suit which they know he'll be cast in; the opposing all Regulation, as against their private Interest, has often been, and daily is complain'd of among themselves.

No wonder, therefore, that the Bankrupt Bill met with such a Treatment, it was in it self unpopular, the Cause of the Weak against the Strong: and they could not lose so fair an Occasion against an Enemy which must one Day have destroyed all Litigious Suits among Traders, and probably have soon introduc'd the *Law Merchant*, which our Neighbours are so happy under, and which, it's amazing a Trading Kingdom should so long have been without.

The Act being thus a Grievance, every Branch of the Law that apprehended any Damage from its Continuance, set on its Destruction, and did soon undermine the Foundation.

The meaning of the Act was made by them to contradict the Design of it; and a Door was left open for the Fraudulent to get out at, and Death, the worst of Deaths prepared for the Honest Man that conform'd to it.

But the Letter of the Law was insisted on, to which there is a high Regard, and which is of such Force, that the Makers only can alter it on the Consequences: But had that been really so, every

every Man would have made use of Patience; and I do not question but Charity would have sustain'd them till the Law was explain'd to help them; but the very Words which were said to be against them were not, *viz.*

Who, after the Twenty Fourth of June, shall become Bankrupt, within the several Statutes made against Bankrupts, or any of them, and against whom a Commission shall be Awarded.

Which I having in part consider'd, shall only observe, That as the Design of the Act was to help the Creditors to the Bankrupt's Estate, and to discharge the Bankrupt, so the Words plainly in its Profits and Penalties took in all Commissions, which after the Twenty Fourth Day of *June* should be Awarded.

And if a Commission is issued after that Day for any Act of Bankrupts committed also after that Day, within any one of the Statutes, which are the very Words of the Act, in which there's no Clause of Incapacity to Exclude them who had committed any Act before from the Benefit, or save them from the Punishment; it's very strange it should pass

pass for a Verbal Interpretation: And what Reason could there be, that a Creditor should not take the advantage of any Act of Bankrupts to be committed by his Debtor, to help him to his Estate, which he could not unless the Debtor might have the Benefit of it; but the Bill being to be destroy'd, they that had the express Words of it on their Side, far'd no better.

The meaning of the Holy Scriptures has been sometimes very differently Interpreted by Men of great Learning and Sanctified Lives, and contrary to the seeming Sence of them; but if the Eyes of the Priest are shut, it's Interest generally shuts them, and Charity it self does not oblige us to think that the Absurdities profess'd by the Romanists, are believ'd by all of them as Truths.

The Clause in the end of the Act was very plain, Every one who were become Bankrupt, and against whom a Commission had issued before the Tenth of *March* One Thousand Seven Hundred and Five, who should voluntarily on or before the Twenty Fourth of *June*, One Thousand Seven Hundred and

and Six, furrender and conform to the Act, should have all the Benefits of it. No Words can be fuller, or more certain; yet several who surrender'd and submitted on the Encouragement of of this Clause, could not get their Certificates confirm'd, and it was in vain to Plead or to Prove that their Commissions had issued before the tenth of *March*, and that they had voluntarily surrender'd on or before the twenty fourth of *June*, as requir'd in the Act, or that they had deliver'd up all they had in the World on the express Words of it.

The Words in the beginning of the Act, which they would think against the Bankrupt, they made much of to condemn him, but when they could not deny but these were for him, they would however Exclude him. If his Commission had not been dealt in for six Months or upwards before the Surrender, they pleaded such Surrenders not good, the Reasons of which I would be glad to know, if they had any; for I would not misrepresent any Person, but give a full Weight to the lightest Pretences; for I had been told before, that in a Penal Law no Meaning could condemn a Man against express Words.

And

And as there was no Proviso, that this Clause should not extend to them, whose Commissions had not acted for six Months, but on the contrary, that it should reach to all against whom Commissions had been awarded before; the Condemnation of them that suffered by it is as hard as the Words are plain, that were to relieve them.

I believe few thought, I sure I did not, that any Person in *England* had a Power of Interpreting any Act of Parliament that shall be made against the express Words of it.

It is certainly a mighty Trust, and I was led into the Belief, that it was too great for any Man, by considering that the Crown it self hath not A Dispensing Power, and it's one of the Blessings of the Revolution, that our Kings can no more claim it.

Before that happy time, we had Lawyers of great Names, and some Judges asserted it, sometimes Necessity, or one thing or another was allow'd as Reason to Interpret the Laws as they pleas'd.

But

But they were learn'd to know themselves, to be Executors of the Law, not Makers of it, and their Punishment remains on Record.

But I must take a further View of the Artillery brought by the Lawyers against the Bill.

When the Words, and the Design of the Act, like Light, dazzled in their Eyes, and that the Bankrupt seem'd past all Danger, they found a Distinction far before our Modern one, of the Spirit and Letter of Treaties so refin'd, that *Aquinas* or *Scotus* might have learn'd of them.

Of Friendly and Adverse Commissions: And its Melancholy Consideration, that the Number of Souls, drove almost to Despair by this Subtilty within this three Months, ten times exceed all who have died by Niceties (which others call Murder'd) from Sir *Walter Rawleigh* to *Algernoon Sidney*; that is to the Act that regulated Tryals for High-Treason: An Act which is justly reckon'd an Honour to the Parliament that Pass'd it, for the fair play it will give even

to

to the Guilty, and the Security to the Honeſt that are unborn. And if ſuch Care was taken of Men that hereafter ſhall be accuſed of the higheſt Crime, to prevent the Innocent's being Sacrific'd by fine Harangues, the poor Souls I mentioned deſerve much more Compaſſion, I will venture to ſay, as the Act knew nothing of Commiſſions being took out Friendly or Adverſe, ſo there was no more reaſon for the diſtinction than Law. And the Pretence that formerly all Statutes were took out adverſe, which in their Sence is againſt the Bankrupt, and that they ought ſtill to be ſo, and now are not, ſeems ſo much a Banter, that if good Manners and Decency were not as exactly to be kept in Writing as in Converſation, and never to be Infring'd, the Provocation would excuſe it.

It muſt be own'd, the Damage that appear'd to be done to the Bankrupts by Commiſſions before the late Act, were more abominable than any have been ſince but it only ſeem'd to hurt the Bankrupt when it fell upon the Creditor; and the many Hundred Pounds ſpent and loſt by Aſſignments, Sittings, and Sales, leſſen'd the Dividends, of which the Bankrupt

rupt had no Share: This those Gentlemen knew, and that no Act of Parliament was ever made to Punish Bankrupts as Bankrupts, but to help the Creditor to his Debt.

Nor do I believe many Commissions have from their first Original been took out with any other Design; the Charge of taking one out is more than most Men will fling away, and if the Bankrupt can hide his Effects, a Commission is seldom took out against him.

Yet it has been earnestly Pleaded, their Commissions are Friendly, or they would have been taken out before the making this Act against them that absconded before; especially if a Relation or known Friend took them out since.

Must the Creditor fling away his Money for nothing, and compliment my Lord Keeper's Officers with the Fees before he knows how to come at any Effects to Pay them? or may he not whenever he finds them out, take out a Commission to come at them? or is it a Bar to any Plea of Debt that the

Plain-

Plaintiff and Defendant are a-Kin?

Surely one Relation may help another; and Nature not only allows it, but pleads for it; and no Nation ever was so Barbarous as to make a Law to the contrary, it's very strange it should be pleaded among us; but what will they not break through to destroy this hated Bill?

There is an Oath to be took, and a Bond to be given to my Lord Keeper, that the Party against whom the Commission is Issued is a Bankrupt, and Indebted to him that sues it forth; which proves his undoubted Right to it, whether he is his Father or his Brother.

But as no Creditor by any former Law was Excluded any means of recovering his Debt, so in this there was nothing like it.

The Legislature, when they punish'd in this Act fraudulent Bankrupts with Death that would not surrender, encourag'd every honest Man to it. They knew every Penny deliver'd by the Bankrupt to his Creditors, which before they could not come at, was so much

much clear Gain; and the Rdeemed Bankrupt added to the Number and Strength of the State; for even Slaves from *Barbary* are thus allow'd to deserve their Ransom.

The Humaine Creditors found their Interest in it, and on Notice that a Debtor was return'd either from beyond the Seas, or appear'd out of their Holes to surrender what they had, made no Difficulty to take out, or renew a Commission, when any thing, tho' but little, was to be got by it.

But you shall not do it with a friendly Design, says the Lawyer, tho' you ever so much prove your self a Creditor.

Good God! Are men to hate to Death? O Charity thou wast never before so used! 'Till now every one honour'd thee tho' they came not up to thy Rules; they bow'd to thy Name that broke thy Laws; they pretended to adore thee, that came not up to thy Divine Precepts; but now thou art disown'd, and Revenge publickly avow'd, in defiance of him, who said it was his own, and he would distribute it.

Plaintiff and Defendant are a-Kin?

Surely one Relation may help another; and Nature not only allows it, but pleads for it; and no Nation ever was so Barbarous as to make a Law to the contrary; it's very strange it should be pleaded among us; but what will they not break through to destroy this hated Bill?

There is an Oath to be took, and a Bond to be given to my Lord Keeper, that the Party against whom the Commission is Issued is a Bankrupt, and Indebted to him that sues it forth; which proves his undoubted Right to it, whether he is his Father or his Brother.

But as no Creditor by any former Law was Excluded any means of recovering his Debt, so in this there was nothing like it.

The Legislature, when they punish'd in this Act fraudulent Bankrupts with Death that would not surrender, encourag'd every honest Man to it. They knew every Penny deliver'd by the Bankrupt to his Creditors, which before they could not come at, was so much

much clear Gain; and the Rdeemed Bankrupt added to the Number and Strength of the State; for even Slaves from *Barbary* are thus allow'd to deserve their Ransom.

The Humaine Creditors found their Interest in it; and on Notice that a Debtor was return'd either from beyond the Seas, or appear'd out of their Holes to surrender what they had, made no Difficulty to take out, or renew a Commission, when any thing, tho' but little, was to be got by it.

But you shall not do it with a friendly Design, says the Lawyer, tho' you ever so much prove your self a Creditor.

Good God! Are men to hate to Death? O Charity thou wast never before so used! 'Till now every one honour'd thee tho' they came not up to thy Rules; they bow'd to thy Name that broke thy Laws; they pretended to adore thee, that came not up to thy Divine Precepts; but now thou art disown'd, and Revenge publickly avow'd, in defiance of him, who said it was his own, and he would distribute it.

Is it impossible for a Man to sue for his own by the Rules of Law, without burning with Malice against the Party he sues? This the Lawyers will not say against their Profession; their Enemies never struck so deep at the Root of their Calling.

Or are not honest fair Traders allow'd to take out Commissions of Bankrupt, as well as commence a Law Suit?

May none take out a Commission to get a part of his Debt, or to make a Legal Title to what his Debtor has to deliver, that is willing to discharge him on so doing?

Or may not an Insolvent, on the Incouragement of this Law, call his Creditors, or the most friendly of them, and tell them his Circumstances, and offer fairly to deliver his Effects to be divided amongst them? Or may not they that were fled beyond the Seas, from the Face of their Oppressors, who would not accept of their Composition, honestly and joyfully return with it to them who were before willing, and desire them to take out a Commission, and accept of their Delivery, which many have

have done, and many are now ready to do: And where lies the Fault? in the declaration of the Bankrupt? or issuing the Commission by the Creditor? or because a Man breaks, and pays not that Fine to the Law which immemorially has been pay'd it?

It must be in the last; for the Creditor might desire to get some of his Debt, and the Bankrupt his Liberty; or to breathe his Native Air, and honestly to get Bread for his Family.

And it would have been very honest, kind and charitable, before so many Surrenders had been made; so many Commissions took out, and so many Families deliver'd their All to the last Farthing, That they had, by publick Advertisement, acquainted the World, that this Act was to be destroyed; and that they declar'd Offensive War against all that were for it, and would enter into the closest Leagues with its Enemies; for what they have done against it would bear a Declaration.

'That whereas an Act pass'd in the
'fourth and fifth Years of Her Majesty's
'Reign, intituled, An Act to prevent

'Frauds Committed by Bankrupts, which
' Act was defign'd to prevent Traders
' going to Law with one another, and
' force the Creditor to accept of what the
' Debtor could pay him, which would
' certainly Ruin great numbers of Law-
' yers who live thereby; and which
' therefore muft be prevented and the
' Act deftroy'd. In order thereunto, we
' do declare, That if any Perfon or Per-
' fons whatfoever, dare to furrender their
' Effects for the ufe of their Creditors,
' they, their Wives and Children, fhall
' be ftarv'd to Death; their Certificates
' fhall be oppofed when they have no
' Money to help themfelves; and fome
' one Act of Bankrupt, which like the
' ftars of Heaven are innumerable, fhall be
' alledg'd fome time or other to be Com-
' mitted by them, to ftop fuch their Cer-
' tificates: And further, for the Encou-
' ragement of all who will go away with
' what they can get of their Creditors,
' they fhall be intirely fecured from any
' Damage; for if they are not Caught
' they are Free; and if they are, they
' fhall not be hurt by it, but may get
' fome Body to prove an Act of Bankrupt
' Committed by them before the Twen-
' ty Fourth of *June*, which Plea fhall be
' allow'd good to all Intents and Purpofes,
' and

'and intirely evade the Punishment de-
'sign'd them by the most pernicious
'Bankrupts Act.

The consequences of their Pleas are so plainly what the foregoing Declaration contains, that they are now as visible as if they had own'd them: They're so often calling it a wicked Act, and coining so many Names for it, and the concern that appear'd in their Eyes and every Action, when they took Notice that formerly Men stood as long as they could, and fought it out to the last Gasp, and that now if they are Arrested, or but threatn'd, a Statute is immediately Whipt out, might like the Anger of some of our Neighbours at the *Scots* Union, open the Eyes of every Considerable Trader, to shew them how much it's their Interest.

For if Lawyers and Attorneys confess they lose Ten Shillings in the Pound, they prove who got it.

And tho' in other Ages it has been Objected, that nothing could pass in Parliament against the Profits of the Lawyers; their Body was so numerous; in our Days we have found even Titles have been settled in *Yorkshire*, which has open'd a Door for the so much wish'd for Register; and my Lord *Sommers* this last Sessions went a great way in the Regulation of the Law.

And since my Lord *Cooper* adorn'd the Bench, without any Law what Alteration have we seen in Chancery? and how glorious already is his Name? and the vast Reputation these two great Men have gain'd, which is the highest reward of Vertue, will put them on to Compleat what remains to be Cured; and Men who have any Modesty left, are ashamed to make any attempts to the contrary, being over-aw'd, tho' not chang'd by their Example.

Now is the time if ever, we may hope, that Justice will Triumph over Eloquence; for how can she plead an unjust Cause, when her Master sits on the Bench, who sees her and will correct her?

It has been further objected against this Bill, that it has occasion'd many wilful Perjuries and secret Evasions to which it will be sufficient to answer if they mean as they say by way of Information,

Were not Bankrupts always examin'd on Oath, and that long before this Bill was thought on, it was Law?

And it is not likely they'll Swear bolder, because the Penalty is increas'd; and that Men will venture the Gallows, who were afraid of the Pillory: The Stating the Fact, is Conviction to the honest and Impartial; but for those that knew before the Methods of Examination, as they have abused all that join'd with them, I shall not trouble my self about them.

They are the Men the Scripture speaks of, whose Tender Mercies are Cruel; and how many have they banter'd to Death with the pretence of it; who pretended the Punishment of the Gallows was too great for Fraudulent Bankrupts, and none would be so cruel as to prosecute them for it; yet found out pretences to condemn Innocent Families to a worse Death, to dye with Want and Hunger, by Invalidating their Certificates, when they had nothing to object against the Truth of their Delivery, by pretending they were not within the Act: And if it's possible any Men can be worse than these, or arrive to a Cruelty

elty more Exalted, let them have the Honour of it, who perswaded their Debtors to surrender and conform to the Bankrupt Act, and deliver all they had to them, and then pretended they were not within it; and may their Names, as was desired by the Incendiary of *Diana*'s Temple, be Recorded to all Ages; for they have reduced some Hundreds to a Condition worse than the Galleys, nay beyond Expression; the Consequences whereof will so certainly and soon be so dreadful to themselves, and such a Reproach to the English Nation, I cannot fear their Enemies can obstruct the Relief they beg for, and which surely they deserve.

For if it's the Interest of the Nation that every Man should be Useful, that our Streets should not swarm with Poor, or our Houses be broke open by what would always break through Stone Walls; surely they deserve Mercy, who, besides the Reason common to other Men, have the Honour of Parliament to plead in their Behalf; for by conforming to their Act this Misery is come upon them.

And it has been the peculiar Happiness of this Nation, and that by which

which they are distinguish'd from all others in the World, that the Representative of the Commons are so great a part of the Legislature.

That August Body have in all Ages, to their Immortal Glory, thought it as much their Business to hear and Redress the Grievances of their Fellow Subjects, as to advance the Nation's Glory, or Exalt by their Supplies the Dignity of their Kings.

And as no Age ever saw a Set of People more Miserable, or a Parliament more Glorious, they must lie at their Feet, and not give over begging till they look favourably on them, and afford them their Help.

They are accused of no Crime, of disobeying any Law; they have fulfilled the end of this, and if any thing in it was worded so obscure that the Judges and the Learn'd Members that help'd to make it could not agree in the Meaning; yet since on such Advice, and presuming on a Parliamentary Security, their Delivery was made; a Security our never to be forgotten King, in his
dying

dying Speech, declar'd none could ever be Losers by;

It's to be hop'd, that a Parliament so sensible as this, of the Advantages he procur'd us, of the Liberty he entail'd on them; will justifie what he said, and grant a Relief to Men Miserable and destitute, Poor and Naked, who approv'd their Honesty at their own Touchstone, and past a Tryal of their own ordaining by an Explaining Clause, or a short Bill, to Enact, 'That all who 'have surrender'd since the making the 'late Act, against the Truth of whose 'Discovery nothing has been made out, 'are within the Meaning of it; and 'that their Certificates shall be imme-'diately Sign'd without Charge: And 'that if they are Molested for any Debt 'owing by them when they made their 'Delivery, on producing such Certifi-'cate, or any Certificate Sign'd, they 'shall be immediately discharg'd.

For as the Woman who in the bitterness of her Soul, when the Famine was in *Samaria*, call'd upon the King against the Woman who had eat part of her Son and hid her own, for which he flung Ashes on his Head and Rent his Cloaths;

Cloaths; even so dreadful is the Cry of the Wives and Children whose Bread is surrender'd to their Neighbours, and who are kept in by the *Assyrians* from getting more.

And I cannot think but with Horrour, that a Bill can scarce pass so soon as to prevent to some a Calamity very like it.

But leaving those Sons and Daughters of Sorrow to them that are both willing and able to help them, it remains for me to offer some Remedies to the Inconveniency that hath been found in this Bill, and which if possible ought to be prevented.

In order to which, and as the Foundation of so great a Good, all false Bottoms must be clear'd, and every one that's not able to pay Twenty Shillings in the Pound should be encourag'd to come in to pay their Creditors what they can, before they make it less; or Ruin others now in a flourishing Condition, by buying of one another to support themselves when they know they cannot pay them.

And

And I need not, to shew this reasonable, either offer to prove, that Men that have nothing can Pay nothing, nor no more of their Debts than their Effects amount to; or that they are more serviceable to the Commonwealth when they work at their Trades, than when they Strole or Steal.

It carries its own Evidence with it, and I have said enough to it already, so shall only give two or three Reasons for appointing a Time for any to come in before the Restriction I shall propose is to take place, who are now unable to pay their full Debts: Provided they make no Payment to any of their Creditors, nor get any new Credit, or in short, receive or pay any Money, but for the support of Life, after any such Bill shall be Enacted. For,

First, As it's very probable that Men that are going backwards will every Day sink what they are now able to Pay, and the Creditors will have the smaller Dividend the longer it is before they make it. So it's for the
Cre-

Creditor's advantage to invite him in, and shew the Encouragement reasonable. And

Secondly, It will be very hard when so much good is like to accrue to Trade, and so much quiet to the Trader, that any who is now in a flourishing Condition should be made otherwise by selling to Men who at present are unable to Pay; for such a Bill, like a fine Net, will catch all that escap'd the Bankrupts Act, which there is reason to believe are but very few.

For considering that Act was look'd on, before *Westminster-Hall* declar'd against it, a certain Relief to all that had ever Broke, or were unable to pay their Debts, from the *Turkey* Merchant to the Ale-draper: It's a happy Proof of the Strength of the Kingdom, when on so general a Muster there were not found above 600 Invalids; and excepting them that are drove to other Nations, who heard not of it soon enough to be yet return'd, the recalling whose Banishment none but Barbarians can be against,

So

So little will be lost in the Pound by them that are yet to come in (those in very ill Circumstances having already Surrender'd for fear the Act should be Repeal'd) that few could be hurt by it, especially if Care was taken to Regulate the Charge of Commissions, which is a much greater Grievance than all laid to the Charge of the Bankrupt, were they true.

Is it not bad enough for the Trader, that he sells to an Insolvent, without being Tax'd to pay the Fees and Charges of Statutes? which are so great, that I have heard of a Messenger that has got above an Hundred Pound by one Commission, and of Attorneys that have made above Five Hundred; besides at least two Acting Commissioners who will neither meet, write their Name, nor do any thing, without a Guinea for each. And it's well known, that several very poor Traders that turn'd all they had into Money, and begg'd up and down for it, could not under Thirty Pound satisfie these Fees.

And if some Method vvas thought on to take avvay, or lessen this Charge, it it would be the greatest Ease and Encouragement ever granted to Trade; and by a very modest Computation, the Creditor loses more by the charge of Commissions, and the method of Sales, than they do by the bad Debts which are made by the Bankrupt. And this Evil, tho' very great, seems as easy to be remedied by some Clause,

' That Commissioners be appointed
' by her Majesty, or the Lord Keeper,
' with stated Sallaries for that purpose,
' Or,
' That the Bankrupt should be oblig'd
' to leave his Books and Papers with
' ——, and File his Accounts before a
' Master in Chancery, with his Affida-
' vit to the Truth of all of them, on
' which he should be clear'd. All which
' at any time to be view'd by his Cre-
' ditors which will be so awful a Tie
' on the ill design'd, that the most da-
' ring will not venture a Conviction for
' which Death is the Punishment.

But it having already been mention'd that there's reason to believe some People have before their going off, made Payments to Friends, in hopes of future Favour, as much to the Da-mage

mage of their Creditors in general, as the private Payments the Bankrupts so much complain they are forc'd to make to satisfie a B. or a T.* when they fall into their Hands.

It may be answer'd, That it were not quite so bad should such Payments be made, for the Humaine and good-natur'd would gain most by such Distinction.

And now its the unmerciful and Inexorable who have above their Proportion. However, such Practices ought by all Means and Ways to be prevented.

But as I have already shewn how strong the Temptation was on the Bankrupts side, who have already surrender'd to this Act, they being left at their last Sitting without any thing to subsist on, till their Certificates came Confirm'd from my Lord Keeper or the Judges, and which Council must be Fee'd to defend But when that is alter'd, the Fea

---

* *Two considerable Traders in Lombard-street alike Famous for refusing all equal Compositions.*

will be remov'd they'll continue to do so: For very few are suspected of it even in the aforemention'd Extremities. And it's much more the Interest of every Bankrupt who hopes to Trade again when he can be clear on his Delivery, to make it fair, and demonstrate his Honesty by a large Dividend of fifteen or sixteen Shillings in the Pound; and he will get many more Friends, and much a better Character by it, than if he clandestinly Pays one and trusts to his Kindness; for the very Man so favour'd will scarcely be so much his Friend, and cannot have so good an Opinion of him that pays him above his Share, as of another whose Delivery is equal; and such Care was taken to prevent any Assignments of Trust, that nothing of that Nature can be fear'd, I had almost said was possible, the Penalties are so high on each side, that they cannot trust one another.

Who will be Trustee for a Bankrupt, and venture himself to be made one, when the Bankrupt for his Pardon and a large Gratuity, may so probably betray him?

If he was a Man of Substance he
stands but on a Precipice, while in
the Power of one, who to his Knowledge was a Villain, tied by no Laws
or Religion; for all things Sacred by
his Fraudulent Delivery he had broke
through.

And a Man of no Substance the
Bankrupt will not trust; for if he puts
his Effects into a poor Man's hand
that wants it as much as himself, how
can he expect the other will part
with it, when he can by no Law
make him, and may be Hang'd for
asking it.

But lest some, in spight of Reason
and Interest, should be still so over-
cunning as to offer at these unequal
Payment, some Clause of Regulation
may be brought in for the future for
all such whose Statutes shall Issue after the time allow'd our present Insolvents to come in, 'which may o-
'blige them within three Months af-
'ter any Loss comes to their Know-
'ledge which will disable them from
'paying their Debts within five Shil-
'lings in the Pound, to Summons their
'Creditors, and deliver them an Ac-

'count of all they have in the World
'for their use, in order to their Dis-
'charge, with a Proviso, That what
'Goods, Debts, &c. they deliver, and
'the Account of what they have so
'lost, or heard to be lost within three
'Months aforesaid, shall together make
'up at least fifteen Shillings in the
'Pound. Thus without apparent Losses no Debtor could mightily hurt his
Creditor; he could not consume his
Effects in Chambering and Wanton-
ness, when oblig'd to make a Discovery to them before he has consum'd
a Fourth of what they intrusted to
him, and his Books would be Vouch-
ers for his Discovery.

This would take off in great measure a very noisy Objection, that Men
may turn what they have into Money,
and swear soundly and keep it.

So they may charge Robberies on Coun-
ties with Ease and little Penalty; yet
how seldom is it practis'd? and I
know very few things too hard for
Villains that will do or swear any
thing.

But in this, Men of Inferiour Trades cannot be suspected; they have seldom much Money thus to play the Rogue with and Men of greater Business cannot easily be guilty of it, if their Delivery and Losses are to make up fifteen Shillings for every Pound they owe; and if they are to come in as soon as they are five Shillings in the Pound worse than nothing. For, such Rogues as these are suppos'd to be, had better run away with all they have, and it will surely be own'd more have done so, and more Mischief thereby, when there was no Law to Punish them, than can be expected will venture their Lives and Liberty when their Delivery must amount so high, and their Books appear regular. As there would be then no frivolous Objections against the honest Delivery, a Delivery that was otherwise would soon be detected.

And as this would encourage and introduce the Practice of Book-keeping, every Man would take Care to keep them exact, than which nothing

Credit *and* Bankrupts.

is more Mathematical, which like some Geometrical Building, if one Stone is took away, all will fall to pieces; and it cannot be expected any Man that keeps Books will begin to keep false Setts of them, in expectation of a future Knavery he may ne'er have occasion for, which besides must all be done by himself; for Clerks and Book-keepers are as Witnesses to Accounts.

But such a Clause cannot reasonably be Enacted without a time allow'd, as I have before propos'd, for every one to come in who are Insolvents; for it would be so much a *post factum* to punish Men for not regularly keeping their Books, when no Law requir'd it; nor was it reasonable it should plainly appear what Losses made a Man Insolvent, till he could be discharg'd on his Delivery of the Remainder left him: But when every one that is Sinking has laid hold of this Clause, and none but clear Traders are left, what *Halcyon* Days must ensue.

It

It will introduce frugality which is so out of Fashion, and put an effectual stop to the prodigious Prodigality and ridiculous Expences, which in this Age do so abound; not only by the Book-keeping aforemention'd, though that in it self, is known to be the best Antidote against the Poison of those Diseases; For our Young Traders must begin the World in another manner, when if they break, they must shew why and wherefore they did so.

If they'll begin Prodigally their Reign can be but very short, when they can spend so small a matter, besides the Stock they begin with.

But few or none will be so mad, for they must consider how such Practises must inevitably ruin them; for if they could not live at first when they had a Fund of their own, they can hope for little Credit when the World knows they have none.

They must daily consult their Books, and see whether their Profits pay their Expences, and they who are not themselves Masters of Numbers will soon learn, or seek for Apprentices or Servants that are; which will more encourage the Educating of our Youth to it; than the benefit of Clergy, allow'd by the Wisdom of our Fore-Fathers as an Encouragement to Letters, did in that Illiterate Age.

Thus should we equal *Holland* in every thing; for Book-keeping, Frugality, and Riches, never go asunder; the first are as seeds to the last, which would thrive here as well as there; and we should as much exceed them in Trade and Wealth, as our Extent of Ground is larger, and our Manufactures and People more Numerous.

The Grandeur of some of our Citizens, would make our Gentry and Nobility be all of them for making their Sons Merchants, if the fall of so many did not fright them, or almost any rose again who fell.

But as such an Act, would Clear and Settle the Accompts of the Unfortunate, every loss would not drive a Trader or a Merchant from his House and Business; for his Creditors would find it their Interest to make up such Losses quietly to preserve his Credit, that they might get it of him again.

Thus the fall of a Bankrupt would be intirely broke, he would be let down so easy, that the Scandal if not the very Name would be lost.

For as that would certainly bring our Young Gentlemen into Trade, their Sisters would intermarry among us, and bring such a Stock, that would cover our Rivers with Ships, and employ every Hand that could Work.

For now Trading is like a Game at Hazard, that the Lucky tye up after a good Run, Purchase an Estate in Land, marry their Daughters with Country Gentlemen; and neither trust them nor their Effects, with Persons whose Bottoms they know nothing of; and who are liable to be undone, by by so many Rubs in the intricate Labyrinth of Trade.

Thus our Stock Ebb and Decrease, little or no Money being brought in. But if this Reproach was took off, our Nobility would prefer Trading to Stock-jobbing, and like it better as the gains grew greater; and the Hazards would soon be no more. For if they were concern'd in Trade, or but Protectors to it, what Incouragement would it have?

It would no longer be complain'd, we have too few Traders in the House of Commons; it would then be every one's Interest, every one would Understand it's Good, and Promote it, Countenance it, and pass Acts in it's Favour.

And we might see the State be publick Insurers; which would be such a Happiness to the Merchant, that his Insurers could not fail; such a Security to the Shop-Keeper, that his Merchant could scarce Break; such Riches to the Kingdom, by preserving our Ships, and their Lading by a double Care,

But

But as the Blessings this will bring cannot be number'd, the Prospect of them are so far off, I shall not at this time give a Calculation how many Ships are Lost, to what are not in time of Peace, and to different Nations; and what Tax on our Export and Import, would probably Answer them: and the difference in time of War.

Or that if the Duties laid on for such Insurance should amount to more or less than what they were design'd, how hey may be alter'd by Parliament, or how the Overplus shall be applied, nor shall I answer any other Objections.

It's as much as I design'd if I have prov'd that the most advantagious helps to Trade will then be granted; or to speak more properly, will come of course: we having nothing else to do but to remove this Stumbling-block, and we shall receive an addition of Strength greater than we hope for from the *Scots* Union.

By that our Strength will indeed increase by the addition of their Hands, for they will be untied; but without a Fund, how little is to be done with them, many Ages have shewn; for they were never charg'd of not improving their means for their Interest.

If our Nobility and Gentry would become one Body with the Trading part of the Nation, and fling in but their loose Thousands which they annually confume in altering or adorning their Houses or Gardens, it would be such a Mass of Treasure, that every Trade would be full stock'd, our Plantations improv'd to a full height; and if Calculation and desire of Gain should take so much Root as to tempt these Gentlemen to a desire to raise their Estates to what once they were in the Days of their Ancestors, I can have no Idea of the Greatness the Nation will rise to; but by considering that *Holland* by the Arts of Trade, though scarce a fifth part as big as our Isle, rose to a Greatness, equal to the mightiest Kingdoms upon Earth, *France* only excepted.

But if any think that Industry may be discouraged, if such Bottoms should Trade; and that Men of Fortune may under-trade others, and be content with small Profit, or with common Interest,

because

because they have something else to live on, by which Men of low Beginning will have no hopes,

It will be sufficient to Answer, that low Interest is so much the advantage of any Nation, and all the World is so convinc'd of it, that the Usurers, or some particular People must submit to the publick good, or complain in secret.

But Industry will by no Means be discourag'd; For Men of Parts, will find more Imployment when there is the most Business, and they will more certainly get plentiful Estates which will more than make amends, tho' they get not so many great ones; for a plentiful Competency is certainly preferable to a *Cæsar aut nullus*, especially with such odds against them as *Experience* daily shews.

That *Mistress* which is the truest Teacher; for she never errs in her Politicks, her Lessons are of the highest value, for they often make up Disappointments, repair the shocks of Fortune, and shew the observing, on what part of the Wheel to lay hold on, and so to manage it, as to prevent its turning.

FINIS.

Postscript.

THE World is at this time so angry with Bankrupts, and so many of the Sufferers by them belong to this great Town; the Complaints against the Men that sought Relief by the Bankrupt Act come from so many Hands, the seem to challenge Belief as due to them; for what every one says must be true. But all I have heard objected, if Gentlemen would be put into a true Light, amounts not to the least Argument against the Bill, but are good ones for it.

'Men have gone off with much, and
'spent it extravagantly, and deliver lit-
'tle or nothing; and it's a Shame to
'see what Rogues spend in the Mint and be-

'beyond the Seas, and how Impudent-
'ly they give an account of it.

Would such Practices have been committed had this Law been in being? Can Debtors do so now? Are these Complaints against them that have Broke since this Law? If not, this Law has regulated all the Mischiefs they complain of, and so demonstrates the goodness of this Bill to all who are not wilfully Blind.

By it already the Mint is destroy'd, which has so often been endeavour'd in vain; the Laws of *Draco* will not always prevail; the Miserable will run some where though a Hundred Acts of Parliament were made against them. When one to lessen their Miseries will attain that end the others cannot.

People run not away with their Creditors Goods, and consume them with their Comrades who are to help to protect them; but willingly deliver them to their Owners, now they have a Law to discharge them. And if some angry Gentlemen would give them-

themselves leave to think, they wou'd find if their Anger is just, for the Money which their Debtors have squander'd away in the Mint, it should appear in the Defence of an Act that has already depopulated it.

But that unruly Passion generally runs the way it ought not; and I have heard of Men of Probity and Reputation in other things, who have in their Zeal against that Place complain'd, they dar'd not attend Commissions of Bankrupts within the Rules of it, for fear of being put in a Wheel-barrow and flung into the Ditch.

Though they knew, none but Bailiffs are ever meddl'd with for coming there; that a hundred Sittings of Commissions have been there, and not a Man insulted.

That it's within the Rules of the Queen's-Bench, out of which Prisoners cannot go; and that others who willingly attended the Commissioners elsewhere, have been took up while doing their Duty, and sent to *Newgate* where they still Lye.

But there needs no more be said of a Place which is made Desolate, and this Act has plainly herein been an Advantage to the Creditor: Is it not so to every Man?

'But are not these abominable Impu-
'dent Rogues? Are such Practices to be
'suffer'd? Do they deserve the benefit of
'any Law?

Many of them deserve nothing, but if they complied with the Law they ought to have the advantage of it; and a hundred scandalous Personal Stories, tho' all true, proves nothing to the contrary; for it's impossible to make any Law, but that more ill Men than good will have Advantage by it.

Nay God Almighty himself, when he would distinguish his People from the *Egyptians*, sent them to *Goshan*; for without it those wicked People would have shar'd in the Blessings of the happy *Israelites*.

'But are such Acounts to be suffered? Yes.

The

The Bankrupt is on Confession, on his Oath, he muſt be Hang'd if his Diſcovery is falſe; and therefore owns what he has done that he ought not.

But if the Gentlemen that complain ſo loud, would take half the Pains to advance Trade as to deſtroy it, I'll lay before them a real Grievance, which if I am the Occaſion by mentioning, of bringing in a Law to redreſs, I ſhall have done my Country ſuch a Service as will be its own Reward, though none of the Hundred Families ſav'd by it ſhould either know or thank me.

There is a Clauſe,

That any Perſon who is Indebted a Hundred Pounds, or more, and ſhall not fatisfie the ſame in ſix Months after it becomes Due, and ſhall be Arreſted, is a Bankrupt.

And the Caſe of Collonel *B-d-ngt-n* anſwers it; he had been ſued in a Debt, which he Tried, it had been ſix Months due, and he pay'd the Money when Caſt, yet he's found a Bankrupt from the time he was Arreſted, and all he did in the mean time made void: his Payments are not good, and many Families muſt be ruin'd by ſuch unexpected refunds;

For long after this, he was in full Credit, a Juſtice of the Peace, on the top of Buſineſs; and I know ſeveral who have receiv'd and pay'd above Two hundred thouſand Pound after they have been Bankrupt within this Statute. By which it's very plain, no Trader in *England* who is not worth more than he anually Returns, tho' that may be Fifty thouſand Pound, but in one Year may be a Bankrupt; he may ſell with much Caution, and perhaps for ready Money, and be never the ſafer; his Cuſtomers tho' very ſubſtantial, may have Money at Intereſt, on Bonds which are due and not demanded, or dormant Notes on different Occaſions, which he by till the whole Accounts are ſetled, or ſomething may be owing on long running Accounts, which are unballanced.

Each

Each of which makes a Man a Bankrupt by this Clause; which I am Credibly Inform'd has not been in use above these three Years, and which on the first Tryal of it, that great Judge of Law, my Lord Chief Justice *H-lt* recommended to the Attorney or Solicitor General, as proper to be repeal'd.

For should all Accounts be unravel'd of Acts of Bankrupts thus Committed Twenty Years ago; if there's no purging them off by living in the same House, following the same Trade, and having fresh Credit, but once a Bankrupt and always so; I may venture to say, that the Fire of *London* did not the Damage to its Citizens; the putting this Law in full force will.

But it will Cause a Million of Law Suits, make up a thousand good Estates to its Practisers; and it begins to be so much used, that every Trader should appear against it, fear it like a Plague, and shew the Parliament it is so, and beg them to repeal it.

If

If this Age is so prejudiced as not to be convinced, how much this Essay is calculated for the Advantage of Trade; I have seen so much Mischiefs for want of something like it, that I don't Question but they'll soon own it, thank me for my good Design, and excuse the Faults which so hasty a Performance laid me under; for which I shall be very thankful, and acknowledge it as full Payment for my Labour.

CPSIA information can be obtained
at www.ICGtesting.com
Printed in the USA
BVHW011055020521
606285BV00014B/922

9 781170 231944